The Six Pillars of Peace

Inner peace – Civil peace – World peace

The Six Pillars of Peace

Inner peace – Civil peace – World peace

Yusuf Mohamed

Edited by

Ammar Alraees

Yusuf Mohamed
2016

First Printing: 2016

ISBN 978-1-365-38292-5

Yusuf Mohamed
P.O Box 22525
Muharraq, Kingdom of Bahrain

yousif.h.y@gmail.com
https://yusufhasanyusuf.wordpress.com/

Dedication

"To whom looking for:

Inner Peace,

Civil Peace,

&

World Peace.

I dedicate this for you!"

Contents

Key to this Book

- This book will guide you to achieve inner peace, civil peace and world peace. Its purpose is to take you on a journey via examples in history.
- It will help us assess some common knowledge axioms all the way till the last page; which will bring you to a realization culminating with this: If you want to achieve inner peace, you really do not have to understand yourself. Quite the contrary, you will have to understand the universe.
- Understanding the world around you keep you calm, patient, strong, confident and thankful. It is Nirvana or at least something close to it.
- You will also discover the secrets of civil peace. It is not about how to control the community through a strong political, financial and security system. It is about understanding people and fulfilling their needs. Being sympathetic will demand respect and collaboration between people from all walks of life.
- You will find that global peace cannot be achieved by ridding the world of its militaries and politicians. It is achieved by maintaining them on the condition that they understand their roles as human beings. Realizing their role in the universe makes people less greedy, more ascetic and productive.

So are you looking forward towards a perfect world?

Perfection! Everyone seeks it but none can achieve it. Is there a standard for perfection? Plato introduced the Utopian concept, which of course did not work Prophet Muhammad (PBUH) stated that: "The best Muslim people are the people who are living now in my century. And then those who follow them. And then those who follow them" He knew that, at the time, there were wars, crimes, and atrocities. But despite that, he said: it is the best. Far from perfect but it is the best.

Perfection does not exist in our universe. The only state of perfection that we know of is God. Nobody's perfect or at least the saying goes, but being perfect does not mean that you are a bad person, quite the contrary.

In fact, working hard to be a better person is your perfect situation. It does not matter how far you reach or how little you achieve. As long as you keep trying to improve yourself, we all will achieve results and great ones at that.

So it goes without saying that world peace will not be achieved if we still think that it can only happen in a perfect world. But it can be achieved in a better and improved world! Together, we can achieve this by knowing the following six pillars of peace

Laying off the armies and security forces

> "As long as armies exist, any serious quarrel will lead to war"
>
> -Albert Einstein

Sometimes, scholars and thinkers get lost trying to find ideal solutions to everyday problems and end up with the most bizarre outcomes. In hindsight, they might not be wrong but the circumstances and the timing would be so off that they would make a bad idea, worse.

Not a single government today would agree with Einstein's quote. If they did with what he is trying to convey, how can they ensure that other governments would follow suit? Costa Rica took some steps towards doing something similar and allocated its national resources to improve their education system. But still they have police! Also they are depending on the army of USA to prevent any foreign threats. At the end, they still have an army providing services when needed!

How can we face threats? How can we impose the rules? Actually, we need two powerful wings: empowerment force and peaceful culture. It seems that you don't need both if you already have one of them, but what will you do if one of them did not work anymore?!

Most people do not see the importance of security forces and blaming them all the time everywhere! No one likes to be body searched in the airports!

Security is an intangible investment. It makes little sense to invest in it until something bad happens. People pay taxes in order to get protected during times of emergency or desperation. Of course, no one wants to experience this level of danger. This is why security awareness is exists, to make sense of all the investments a nation makes in terms of security; and it is because of these investments that most nations in the world live in peace.

Security awareness talks about having your countermeasures to prevent any incident. While peaceful culture lets you sleep at night without locking your house door, leaving your car unlocked and enter the supermarket or misplacing your wallet or mobile phone in a restaurant and finding it later at the same place. I have experienced this in Bahrain, once upon a time. Do you think this is more attractive than the prizes of war? I do.

Founding Utopia

Building a perfect house requires perfect materials, furniture and tools which do not change or get old. A Utopian society requires perfect people whose moods do not change. Their brains never think about breaking rules and they all maintain a permanently positive temperament. This will never, ever happen in our lifetime. If you think that you have met the perfect person, I am sorry to say that you did not see the full picture of him/her. This is the proof: As long as this person gets more knowledge and experience every new day, it means this person was not perfect yesterday!

Perfection means nothing is missing. You cannot add anything to it. At a personal level, nobody is perfect but there are perfect situations. Same applies to the social level.

There are no bad people, only bad mentalities. Since we expect bad deeds or attitudes to stay with most of us, we should have our own self-correcting mechanism to deal with them. This is why punishment by the state was invented in the first place. Today, it comes in the form of financial penalties, jail or capital punishment. Whatever it is, it must be fair. Moreover, as we understand that nobody is perfect, we should expect that any human may do wrong things, whoever they may be or whatever position they hold.

So what is the perfect situation at the social level? People with bad habits or mentalities are more expected to do wrong things. But leaders and scholars may do so too! Understanding this fact is part of the perfect situation. The other part is to understand that everyone can be changed for the better. Ours is a forgiving God, so who are we to not forgive people's faults?

To recap on the above, note these as points to understand going forward in life:

The Six Pillars of Peace

1. Nobody is perfect
2. We should understand the fact that everybody is able to change for the better
3. We should accept those people who are working hard to be better people

Infinite Success and Infinite Failure

In the business world, some organizations are classified under as "too big to fail". If you believe in that statement, take a moment and compare those organizations or rich families and try to remember how they were just years ago. You may find some of them were small but ambitious. And you may find some of them did not even exist! If you still believe in that statement, be sure that they themselves do not believe in it! That's why they still plan, work and move forward.

Believing they are too big to fail will only lead them to failure They might want you to believe in it in order to protect their organizations but they will never believe in it themselves. This makes smaller organizations demotivated to compete with bigger organizations.

This world keeps changing, as day and night, hunger and satiation, happiness and sadness. It is the Yin Yang effect. If you are living in a conflict zone, know that conflict cannot last forever. If you are living in a peaceful place, know that warlords will not let it stay that way for long.

Likewise, at a personal level, if you are in a bad mood, it is not the end of the world! Also, if you are in a good mode, silly things will reverse your state, making you nervous and sad. It's not about how to avoid these changes, it's about how to deal with those changes, how to protect yourself and change in a smart way.

Just believe that nothing remains as it is. We all should have the willpower to be part of positive change, at all levels. (Find the details of this subject in my book "The compass". Also search for "The Triangle of Change" in Wikipedia)

Absence of the Enemies of Success

As a positive person, you should ask yourself: Do negative people exist? We mentioned earlier that there are no bad people, just bad habits. So why do some people stop others from doing the right things? Why do they take it upon themselves to act as barriers to stop people achieving their dreams, goals and peace?

The reasoning behind this bizarre act is that global peace, civil peace, your inner peace; dreams and goals are conflicting with their benefits, nay their very existence in an organization or even the world! When we talk about barriers we always think about our competitors first and that is normal. In fact, competitors are working hard to be better than you but they don't try or even think how to stop you dreaming. Other people do! They might even be your friends or loved ones.

By slightly entering another's comfort zone, you will find a big war will be waged against you. You will find yourself to be an unacceptable person in your own society because you broke their rules, traditions and conventions.

In this case, I am offering you three options:

1. Either choose being with them or with your dream. I don't recommend this as the best option but you may be forced to take it sometimes.
2. Try to balance between them and your dreams. You may not make them very happy but you will achieve 50% of your dreams. This will work for a while but then you will have to either go back to the first option or take the third option.
3. Make them understand you more. Explain what is your vision and what you strive to do. This will help you in turning them from barriers to partners. You will gain a lot of them, but not all of them. And this is what I see as best practice.

There are few more barriers: bitter and envious people. Don't even think about them. They are only harming themselves and their health. They cannot be competitors, but some competitors are downgrading themselves and becoming bitter and envious with a little power which might harm you if you are not careful. Think of them like a little water which may cause your two- ton car to slip and put you in danger if you are not careful. Vigilance is key.

Why am I saying they are dangerous but small? Because if they were big enough to be your competitors, they will never feel threatening. They know their own weakness and they see the fact from inside. Never doubt their existence because they will be always around you! Don't worry, just relax, be careful and move forward. Small fry will always be small fry.

Lack of opportunities to form alliances

With the surrounding competitors / enemies in your world, it is normal that you feel alone, weak and threatened; however, you always can turn people from enemies to alliances, from competitors to partners.

If you fail to turn someone into a partner, shift to another one and try again! Keep chasing partners till you accumulate them like weapons in your arsenal. Keep in mind your partners are not like you. They should be different but compatible with your personality. They should believe in you, and you should believe in them. You both should believe in one vision and believe that you are the best current option as a partner for the long-term. Believe that you can protect each other's benefits and existence. That is what makes the European Union exist till date! They speak many different languages, they have different economic practices, religious thoughts and philosophies. But they feel that they need to unite. This makes each partner stronger. The moment they feel that it does not protect their benefits and existence, it will be dissolved. The same applies to NATO, the GCC etc.

Why don't you make your own union? Just share your power with others who can do the same for you. There must be something mutually beneficial between you. The point is: there must be potential alliances, you have to find them. And the most important thing is: you can make anybody an ally or friend simply by sharing power and benefits.

HINT

Events keep happening in the universe. I am not talking here about the movement of the earth around the sun or physics. Our subject here is peace, all types of it: inner peace, civil peace and global peace. Through the hints in this book, we will explain things which keep happening among people which should makes you understand this universe, your community, this book and yourself much better.

Take it very seriously!

The Arms Race

Before a cheetah chases a deer, the cheetah watches its prey, runs, attacks and ultimately kills and eats its prey. The deer on the other hand tries it best to stay vigilant, careful and fast to react and run away. Both are prepared for a reason: to survive. But each one has a different vision, different power and different way of thinking and preparation.

It is acceptable when we talk about preparation for being protected. Survival is a very valid reason! We can apply this to animals, humans and even plants!

When we talk about mankind, we can understand that everyone, nation, organization or state is working hard to get protected and this is a valid reason to build an army or internal security system or even hire a special lawyer.

What is not acceptable is using protection tools for violating the rights of others: the right to freedom and the right of survival. Be strong enough in order to protect yourself, not to attack others. Being strong will deter others from initiating a war against you.

But, if you are sure that if you do not initiate attack then you will be under attack, what should you do? Simply, attack! You are on the front line of defense! Ensure that they lose their attack tools, not their protection tools, because it is their right.

Crime and terrorism

What is the difference between a criminal and a terrorist? Criminals are more motivated to act for monetary gain or personal issues. They are unpredictable and it's difficult to classify them. On the other hand, terrorists are more motivated to act against governments. They work to gain international attention and publicity for their cause. They operate in small groups or complex networks and are usually well trained. They always have access to necessary resources such as money, technical knowledge, weapons, explosives, and sometimes supported by governments; because their aims are often political in nature.

A question might rise in your mind: can the criminal be a terrorist? Answer is NO! Terrorists have principles while criminals do not. But they both might have short term collaborations. It is very dangerous and we should be smart enough to deal with this issue. Simply by realizing that as long as we live on this planet, they will continue to exist with us. There will be always good opportunities to turn some of them to good, law-abiding people. This makes them weak! There will be always good opportunities to keep them fighting against each other instead of fighting with you!

Existence of New Power and the Fall of the Older Guard

The shining stars, be they your boss at work, friend, favorite team, the most powerful bank or even your own nation, are affected by factors which make them rise or fall. All the shining stars are going through start up stage, maturity and then recession. So the shining stars today may not shine tomorrow.

Don't let that upset you but be prepared to be harmonized with the new shining star in your life. Don't think that the new current star will stay at peak brightness forever. As the angel Gabriel told the Prophet Muhammad: "love whoever you want to love, but keep in mind that, one day, you will be separated" There are many reasons for this separation.

This will make you balanced at recession time and you will be able to think and act in a good, practical and brave way.

The Enemies of Success

You will never make them friends and will never beat them. They are not your personal enemies, competitors or friends. They just decided mindfully that they should hate any kind of success. You will always hear, read and come cross their attempts to downplay any success story. They are what we call, “losers”.

If you are honest enough to the people you are targeting, you can easily ignore those losers. If you are not honest and clear to your target population, they can easily paint you in a negative light and give people a very bad impression about you. They just need some time to break you. Just be honest with yourself, create your vision and acts very clearly with others.

Possibility of gaining alliances

The main power of any start up is will power. You may not have any kind of support but that will not last forever. You may suffer for a long time trying to find the suitable environment for yourself or your organization.

One of the elements of your success will always be "your partners". As we said before, if you look for them, you will find them. And be sure that someone somewhere will be glad to share his worth with you in order to keep his assets valuable and get some benefit from your valuable assets too.

If you are a new power in this world, your future partner might be an enemy in the beginning. This helps him to understand you more. If you couldn't show yourself clearer, don't blame them if they can't understand you!

The possibility of gaining them is always there and is always dependent on you.

HINT

In business, history, politics, sports and technology; once something better comes up, the rest will fall! It is logical and simple!

You have to always keep in mind that you, your community, party, entity or nation may fall if another comes up with a better concept, product, service or idea.

People with bad habits will work hard to ensure that no one betters them and takes away what they think is rightfully theirs. It does not matter to them if they did it the right way. This situation is the crux of society today, delaying the development of mankind, nations and communities.

People with good habits will accept this rule in a positive way: they will work hard on development and continuous improvement in order to ensure that they keep themselves and their world as improved versions of their former selves.

Things you Can't Avoid

Betrayals

Betrayals are a fact of life. They occur on a personal level, community level or even national level. It is the violation of your critical information. The challenge is to decide what part of your information should be out there, with whom you to share it and when.

You should share it only with people who can help you in achieving your goals. This goes in some ways against social media which encourages people to post their life for all to see and document. What is the value of the content you are providing to others around you? Moreover, are you getting any benefit out of it or is it being used against you? Think deep before you open your Pandora's Box to someone.

Regarding information security on an organizational level, Non-Disclosure Agreements (NDAs) solve the biggest part of this challenge.

But we have a challenge here: Each organization has its own secrets. And each level in the organization holds different type of secrets. How can we share the upper level secrets with lower level staff for the purpose of orienting them and preparing them for future promotion or leadership role?

We are talking here about shaping a second generation of management in the organization who can adapt the vision and take over the responsibilities. Here, the HR holds the "How to" knowledge. It is about the proper earlier process of selection, recruitment, training and evaluation. It is an old concept that was taken from Islamic Sufism.

Being tracked by Enemies

What if we didn't protect our information? Despite the fact that most of it is not critical, some people have their eyes on you or your organization, watching for your mistakes, gaps or sorting your information in a way which could reflect badly on you. It might be fake or real, it doesn't matter as long as it is affecting you negatively.

It is very difficult to minimize your released information but you should be always aware of protecting your critical information. What is critical information? Well, as a first step, you should classify your information as critical and non-critical. It depends on you and how big or small your private circle is. People living in the city call people living in the next flat "neighbors" while people in the desert calls the others living in a tent five kilometers away "neighbors" too. It's all about you, the size of your private circle and how you classify the things around you.

The most important thing is that you should not keep yourself in a gray area. Be white or black; otherwise do not blame anyone if they believe whatever they hear about you.

Moreover, you may find rumors about you despite that you were very clear in your vision and method. But this will not take too long to be discovered as lies and fabrications because you were prepared!

Be like a professional manager, financial controller or accountant who is ready to be audited by an external entity. In Islam, it's called "Ihsan" which is defined as: "worshiping God as if you are looking at Him. If not, so worshiping God as you know that He is watching you!" how do you work when your manager or supervisor is watching you? Do you keep yourself in gray areas?

Increases in cost

There is a time challenge associated with every idea. With passage of time, the cost of implementing this idea will increase. It will either be at the expense of your personal development level, family, community level or even governmental level.

If this idea is about your priorities, then make sure that you do it on time. Or find a partner if you feel that time is not on your side. Or, just leave it! You may do it in the future with higher cost. But, at that time, you should have enough resources to do it. So stop thinking how to do it now, this will not make you forget about your aspirations. Instead, it will help you to focus on how to grant enough resources to do it in the future.

For the time being, you should think about the action that will lead you to the next step.

Surprises

First, always make a plan for everything in your life. Second, have a plan B with flexibility to accept any unexpected changes. Once you keep that in mind, you will remain calm because you are prepared to accept changes.

It's not necessary that you get 100% prepared for "unexpected changes" because some surprises come from outside the box unlike the expected threats or risks. However, accepting facts, patience, flexibility and your clear powerful motivating vision will help you to manage your crises.

What we are not talking about here is your plan A because you know what you want to do better than anyone else. I am writing here to inform you what plan B should contain:

First of all, plan B must aim to achieve the same goal of plan A. Otherwise it will be considered as plan A for another goal! For example: if you failed in your leasing cars business, you may have run a successful bakery business which was your traditional family business. The goal here is not having a successful leasing cars company. The goal here is getting rich!

Second, plan B must have a buffer for the surprises which should help you to minimize its effects on you. Operationally, always keep a possible back step. Financially, try to have savings. Or at least, try to have a very good credit history in order to have the ability to get loans whenever you need.

You will face a lot of bad surprises. But pleasant surprises exist too, and plenty of them!

Hope

> "There is no despair with life, and there is no meaning of life with despair"
>
> -Mustafa Kamil

Hope, not only keeps you strong, it makes you think more and more of a way to your own success. Hope makes you understand your failure as a valuable lesson; Like a dose of caffeine which makes you see your goal clearer and realize other practical alternatives.

Simply, you have two options after any failure: move forward till you achieve your goal or find an alternative to achieve success.

HINT

There's an old adage that says, 'Good times come only after bad times'. You would not enjoy the sweetness of success if you did not experience the bitter road to get there. During any hardship, there is a gift from God. Find it!

Things you Must Avoid

Pointing fingers

Pointing fingers without evidences never solves any problem. Did the United States find any weapons of mass destruction in Iraq after its occupation? Pointing fingers is a very dangerous attitude which is usually followed by very serious repercussions.

This may lead to a severing of relations, being in jail or death of at least one person! And this is not a small issue! Prophet Muhammad (PBUH) said: “demolishing Kaabah (the black building in Mecca) is a smaller issue than killing a believer!”

This bad attitude can be a result of a criminal mentality or can be a result of any kind of xenophobia (against Muslims, Blacks, Russians, Persians, you name it!)

Generally, mankind has a strange unfair judgment attitude. For example: An Algerian French boy grew up in France. He has an Islamic name, Zinedine. He loved soccer and joined a football club and became a very successful player. He also played a vital role in the 1998 World Cup when France became the world champions at that time. Every French person was proud of him. Everyone acknowledged that Zinedine is a great person.

What if this boy was not dedicated to his hobby? What if he gave up facing racism in France and did not become a soccer player? What if he grew up with gangs and became a criminal or worse yet, a terrorist?

People will not say “Zinedine is criminal” or “terrorist”. Usually they don’t link the sins to the person who did it; they always link it to his group. And in this case, they may say: “Muslims are terrorists” or Immigrants are criminals” or “you can’t trust Algerians and any other Arabs”

Sins belong to the person who committed them, or to the group of people who were involved. Likewise, achievements belong to the person who did them, or to the group of people involved.

Promoting the enemies

Public circulation of your competitor's news and information is very sensitive and must be dealt with very carefully.

When you feel that you need to talk about them, or have to mention them, make sure that you don't promote them or it will be a clear public message to everyone that they are better than you. Especially if people found later that what you are telling about thcm is not %100 true.

This is pushing people to get more close to them in order to know them more. And then, they may get familiarized more with them until they become a preferred choice over you. This is happening in the US elections race as we speak.

So, know your enemy or competitors as you know yourself. Then you can give the people their true picture.

Reducing costs by reducing the quality

"The need is the mother of all inventions"

-Arabic proverb

Never do that. You might think to do it to maximize your profit or minimize your losses. But actually, you are losing your most valuable asset, your credibility.

In fact, there are other ways to face this type of financial challenge. If it is related to the sales challenge, you may challenge the greed and reduce your margin!

If it is related to the expenses challenge, you may look at the details of the expenses and decide what you actually need at this stage and what you really don't need.

Inventing new products, ways or ideas may increase your earnings with better conditions in term of cost or margin. Just try to find your way, your invention!

Putting priceless things at risk

There are things that you must not put at risk. We mentioned credibility earlier. The moment you lose it, you will lose your value. So many other things such as family, relations and principles are priceless.

What if priceless things are becoming barriers in front of your success path?

Don’t ever put your priceless assets at risk but stick to your goals because you are going to achieve them one day. Even if you are in the process of doing it, you should always make sure that you keep your priceless assets with you till the end of your life.

Achievements are not worth anything if you cannot share them with anyone. It is even worse when you forego your principles and values on the way.

Frustration

Are you thinking of giving up? It's up to you, but take few moments before you make that decision.

In this stage, I would advise you to take a step back. That does not mean it's the end of the story. We are human, we may feel down and it's an indicator informing us that something went wrong.

Step back and it will help you see the full picture. And then, you will see what went wrong. You may realize that you need to activate plan B or to seek advice from someone who can open new horizons in your imagination factory.

Frustration should help you as an indicator, not to make you give up. It's your choice!

HINT

There is no end to greed! Also there is no end of ambition too. But the difference between them is you.

Ambition makes you a noble person while greed makes you an ignoble person. Choose your path wisely.

Your start line!

Whatever is your current condition, and decided to start, you may start from exactly where you are! Don't wait, don't postpone and don't think that there is a start line where everyone must stand on first. Your start line is where you stand now, or sit, or lay down!

First, understand your universe and the purpose of your existence. Understand the people; consider where they came from. Understand yourself and be very honest with yourself.

Second, protect your value as a human being. Respect yourself and don't allow yourself to lose your value as a human by your acts. Respect others and don't accept any insult or harm.

Convey to this understanding, convey to respect and unify the vision towards peace.

It always starts from down to up, keep it up!

> "You will not enter Paradise until you believe, you will not believe until you love each other. Would you like to know how you can love each other? Spread peace among you"
>
> -Prophet Muhammad (PBUH)

HINT

Compared to the end result, all beginnings feel weak and feeble. Don't expect that you should get the proper support and resources to start. Start, even if you are weak. Most of the great successful people and organizations were actually very weak. I am sure that you came across some of them.

Since "need" is the mother of invention, weakness is the seed of success. The moment you become arrogant or cocky and think that you are the greatest, you will fail!

The greatest is God!

The End

As everyone starts different from each other, ends also are different. You may achieve inner peace, civil peace, world peace or any other goal. But you may not! You may stop for any reasons: death, sickness or any other new priorities that recently stood in your way. You should be satisfied with what you did as long as you did your best, even if you did not achieve your target. The effort is part of your success Enjoy the trip before you enjoy the destination. Deliver your vision to others so they can continue the journey from where you stopped progressing. Then, you may live in peace or rest in peace.

Back to where we started with: inner peace is achieved through Nirvana. Civil peace is achieved through Sympathy. World peace is achieved through Asceticism.

****

Nirvana – Sympathy – Asceticism

****

****

****

******

***

*

Author Bio

Yusuf Mohammed is an Aviation Security Expert who found himself as an inspirational writer. He introduced "The Triangle of Change" in his book "The Compass" which explains how people, societies and organizations are having a positive or negative change.

Although he is travelling around the world to train Aviation Security, he takes this opportunity to promote peace too.

www.ingramcontent.com/pod-product-compliance
Ingram Content Group UK Ltd.
Pitfield, Milton Keynes, MK11 3LW, UK
UKHW041834200726
13854UKWH00003BA/1137

9 781365 382925